up high

10:God

down smart.

Joseph

SSSS

GOD

dear God

HEAVEN on EARTH

ZONDERVAN®

ZONDERVAN

Dear God
Copyright © 2010 by André K. Dugger

Requests for information should be addressed to:

Zondervan, *Grand Rapids, Michigan 49530*

ISBN 978-0-310-32773-8

Cover design: Extra Credit Projects
Cover photography: Dale Stroud and Bob Scott
Interior photography: Dale Stroud and Bob Scott
Interior design: Steve Culver

Printed in China

10 11 12 13 14 15 • 12 11 10 9 8 7 6 5 4 3 2

This book features letters to God written by
eight-year-old Tyler Doherty, who suffers from
cancer, as well as from others in Tyler's life who
write letters to God.

Each letter is followed by words from
the Bible and a short reflection on the meaning
behind the letter.

Perhaps reading this book will encourage you to
write your own letters to God.

letters to God

A MAJOR MOTION PICTURE

Inspired by a true story, the movie *Letters to God* features lead character eight-year-old Tyler Doherty. Tyler lives in a small town with his widowed mother Maddy, his teen-aged brother Ben, and his grandmother Olivia.

Tyler suffers from cancer but is in good spirits in spite of his ongoing chemotherapy treatments. Tyler talks to God on a regular basis by writing letters and sending them to God via U.S. mail.

Although letters to God, Santa, and the Easter Bunny are routinely shredded at the local post office, Tyler's letters to God intrigue the mailman on Tyler's route and rather than discarding them, he turns them over to his supervisor who reads them and decides to hang onto them.

When the mailman on Tyler's route needs to take two months off, the postal supervisor assigns a substitute—Brady McDaniels. Brady, a down-and-out divorced father, gets to know the people on Tyler's street, including old Mr. Perryfield and young expectant mom Mrs. Baker who has an over-protective guard dog and whose military husband has been deployed to Iraq.

In spite of Tyler's ongoing illness he attends school and spends a lot of time with his best friend, Samantha. Tyler regularly writes to God about his friends, family and days at school.

Mailman substitute Brady asks his supervisor what to do with Tyler's letters to God and is told to decide for himself. He decides to take the letters to a church which happens to be the church home of Tyler and his family. The pastor says God wants Brady to have the letters.

As the story unfolds, Brady and Maddy (Tyler's mom) become friends and Brady, through reading Tyler's letters and getting to know the Doherty family, comes to know Christ.

Although Tyler's cancer finally takes him home to heaven, the influence of his letters to God activity spread to his schoolmates, his neighborhood and beyond as many others learn to share their deepest needs by writing their prayers as letters to God.

Dear God,

How many people are in heaven?
Must be a lot. I know two and
I'm only eight.

Love, Tyler

In my Father's house are many rooms; if it were not so, I would have told you. I am going there to prepare a place for you. And if I go and prepare a place for you, I will come back and take you to be with me that you also may be where I am.

John 14:2-3

How many people are in heaven? Have you ever wondered? Only God knows how many people are in heaven now and how many will be in heaven for all eternity.

His assurance for you in this Scripture passage is that Jesus, God the Son, not only is preparing a place for you in heaven, but also will come back and take you to that place with him.

The important thing is to know that God loves you and he has provided a way for you to be in heaven. His greatest desire is for you to have a relationship with him forever. If you have received Jesus as your Lord and Savior, you are going to be there, and you need to tell others how they can be sure they will be there too.

Dear God,

I learned a new word today. Medu...llob... Lastoma. Something. My mom says I'll be sick for a while but it'll be OK. She said it wasn't anything I ate.

Love, Tyler

He has made everything beautiful in its time. He has also set eternity in the hearts of men; yet they cannot fathom what God has done from beginning to end.

Ecclesiastes 3:11

Peace I leave with you; my peace I give you. I do not give to you as the world gives. Do not let your hearts be troubled and do not be afraid.

John 14:27

Sometimes people get sick. We don't know why some people get cancer and others don't, nor do we know why some die young and some live well into old age. Life and death are in the hands of God.

We do know that God is a loving God and that he has a great plan for each of us. God's plan is not only for our time on this earth, but also for eternity. God is able to comfort us with his peace that far exceeds the temporary peace the world has to offer.

Live in God's supernatural peace so others may see how to do the same.

Dear God,

Why am I sick God? The medicine stinks. But I don't have to take my spelling test this week so that's good.

Love, Tyler

. . . I have learned to be content whatever the circumstances.

Philippians 4:11

In life there are times when we experience things we don't enjoy.

We have two options for how we will respond; we can either become angry and hard or we can become thankful and tender.

The hard-hearted person is the person who focuses on the negatives of their life and is full of anger, resentment, and bitterness.

The tender-hearted person is the person who focuses on the positives of their life and is overcome with thanksgiving.

Whatever the circumstance, we can focus on God and his blessings rather than the negative problems around us. Learn to live with a contented spirit no matter what occurs in your life.

Dear God,

Can you see the stars from heaven? My dad said you made them all. I'm really glad to be home from the hospital.

Love, Tyler

God made two great lights — the greater light to govern the day and the lesser light to govern the night. He also made the stars. God set them in the expanse of the sky to give light on the earth, to govern the day and the night, and to separate light from darkness. And God saw that it was good.

Genesis 1:16-18

He determines the number of the stars and calls them each by name.

Psalm 147:4

As we face struggles in life, we need to remember how awesome and how majestic God is.

Consider the fact that God made everything that exists. He made the stars in the sky and he even knows them by their names. If God can call the billions of stars he created by name, he certainly knows your name.

Rest in the assurance that God knows you and loves you. Take the time today to reflect on the incredible glory of God.

Dear God,

But most of all, I really just wish my mom would laugh. I miss that the most.

Love, Tyler

Our mouths were filled with laughter, our tongues with songs of joy.

Psalm 126:2

When someone we love is hurting, we desire for them to experience God's joy again and to be able to laugh and enjoy life.

God can bring happiness, but even more important, he can place joy into our heart. Only God can allow us to experience an abundant life.

Receive the joy God has available and help others discover that same joy through Christ.

Dear God,

My first day back at school was very exciting. I forgot to tell Sam to do what Jesus would do. We all ended up in the principal's office to sort things out.

Love, Tyler

To this you were called, because Christ suffered for you, leaving you an example, that you should follow in his steps.

1 Peter 2:21

Sometimes in life we face difficult situations and experience times of suffering.

Jesus experienced difficult times in life and he suffered greatly as he died on the cross.

Just as Jesus continued to demonstrate love to others throughout his trials he calls us to do the same.

When a difficult situation comes along, think and pray before reacting. Ask, "How can God be glorified in this situation? How would Jesus react to this situation?"

Jesus left us an example of unconditional love; even in extremely distressing circumstances. If he is living in us, we have the same power to love and overcome any situation that he has. We should strive to live in such a manner that Jesus will shine through us every day.

Dear God,

My mom came for me and Sam.
I'm not sure who she was more
worried about, Sam or me.

Love, Tyler

As a father has compassion on his
children, so the LORD has Compassion
on those who fear him;

Psalm 103:13

When someone you love is dealing with a trial of some kind, it is natural to be concerned about that person.

Our heavenly Father is concerned for us and he demonstrates his love for us on a regular basis.

As humans, sometimes our concern becomes worry and that is something God wants us to avoid. Rather than worrying, we need to allow our concern to be translated into prayer as we lift up the one for whom we are concerned. We should be thankful that God and others care for us. We should also demonstrate our love for others by praying for them.

Dear God,

On the way home Mom tried to be very firm but when Sam told her how potatoes were stuck up Alex's nose, she laughed and laughed. Now I know you're getting my letters -cause only you could figure out a way to make her laugh.

Love, Tyler

Sarah said, "God has brought me laughter, and everyone who hears about this will laugh with me."

Genesis 21:6

God is able to bring laughter to a heart that is hurting
and joy to lips that have cried out with pain. There are
times in life when we are overwhelmed with grief and
heartache. In times like these we need to be able to
laugh again.

God is able to restore laughter to hearts that have been
filled with sorrow. We should take the time to carry our
loved ones to the Lord in prayer and trust him to bring to
them the answer that is needed.

Praise God that he can restore a broken heart and once
again bring the joy of laughter.

Dear God,

We got home just when the mailman was at our house. I guess all the excitement got to me 'cause I threw up on his shoes.

My mom couldn't believe it. All she could do was laugh.

Love, Tyler

. . . a time to weep and a time to laugh, a time to mourn and a time to dance

Ecclesiastes 3:4

Learn to laugh; it sure beats crying all the time.

Scripture makes it clear that there is certainly a time to cry in life. The truth is, we will experience many times in life when we will cry, but we will also experience times when we will laugh.

Look for humor even in the negative things that happen. We can focus on either the negative or positive things of life; the choice is ours.

Spend time today looking for opportunities to laugh in the most unusual of places. Sometimes it is in the midst of situations that normally result in weeping that God provides the gift of laughter.

Choose to laugh today and choose to help others do the same.

Dear God,

All in all God, it was a very good day.

Love, Tyler

This is the day the LORD has made;
let us rejoice and be glad in it.

Psalm 118:24

Learn to live with a commitment to make the most out of every day God provides.

When we expect to experience a bad day we will often find a bad day waiting for us. When we expect to experience a good day we will often find a good day waiting for us as well.

Everybody has bad things happen to them and everybody could make a list of issues to complain about.

Each person could also make an extremely long list of things for which they should be thankful.

Rejoice; the Lord has given today as a gift. Make the most of today by focusing on the positives God has provided.

24

Dear God,

There's so much pain in my daughter's heart. She's moving away from You. Lord, that little boy needs to see her faith, her trust in You.

Love, Olivia

But those who hope in the LORD
will renew their strength.
They will soar on wings like eagles;
they will run and not grow weary,
they will walk and not be faint.

Isaiah 40:31

27

Everyone places his or her hope and trust in someone
or something.

God is the only one worthy of our faith and when we
trust him like we should, we are blessed and we are
an encouragement to others as well. When our hope is
placed in the Lord we are renewed in our strength and
we are able to face whatever comes our way.

We must learn to place our hope and faith in the Lord and
encourage others to do the same.

Dear God,

I'm writing this only because my brother asked me to. He thinks it'll help. I don't see how. I've lost everything. All the big stuff like my dad and now with Tyler being sick, all the normal stuff: like going to hockey games and having cookouts.

Love, Ben

Praise be to God,
who has not rejected my prayer
or withheld his love from me!

Psalm 66:20

Sometimes we just need to vent. That is okay!

God is big enough to handle our prayers with all of our honesty and transparency. As a matter of fact, God desires for us to share our heart with him openly and honestly. He is already aware of our feelings and experiences. He wants us simply to come to him and share our heart.

God desires for each of his children to come to him in humble, honest prayer and he will never reject that kind of communion. We need to openly share our heart with God and help others learn how to do the same.

Dear God,

Can't Tyler just get better? I know my mom loves me but sometimes I think she wishes it was me sick and not Tyler. And who can blame her?

Love, Ben

I praise you because I am fearfully and
  wonderfully made;
your works are wonderful,
I know that full well.

Psalm 139:14

One of the greatest gifts we have been given from God is the gift of prayer.

When someone we love is sick we should go to God in prayer for them and ask God to heal them.

At times we may feel as though we are not as worthy of love as someone else is. When we begin to experience feelings of inadequacy and unworthiness, we need to remember how much the Lord loves us and all he has done for us.

We could spend the entire day naming blessings God has bestowed upon us and not begin to scratch the surface of all he has done.

If we ever doubt how much God loves us we simply need to remember how he gave his Son Jesus to pay the penalty for our sins. We should picture Jesus as he stretched out his arms to willingly be nailed to the cross for us. Never forget that each of us has been fearfully and wonderfully made by God and are deeply loved by him as well.

Dear God,

I feel yucky today, but Sam really wants to climb trees. I already threw up three times this morning though. Sam's going to need another friend you know—someone who likes to climb trees. Her grandfather is a lot of fun but I don't think he can climb trees.

Love, Tyler

> Look to the LORD and his strength; seek his face always.
>
> Psalm 105:4
>
> A friend loves at all times . . .
>
> Proverbs 17:17

There are times in life when we are so sick and weak that we do not have the strength to participate in the basic activities of life.

The blessing for the believer is that the strength of the Lord is always available for us.

One way God strengthens us is through friendships. Friendship is one of God's greatest blessings. True friends are there for us whether we are strong or weak, sick or well, happy or sad. True friends are used by God to encourage us and bless us when we are experiencing a valley in our life.

God also blesses us by allowing us to love, bless, and encourage our friends. It takes total reliance on God's power and strength to do that when we don't feel like it. We need to live focusing on the power of God and appreciating those special people God has placed in our life called friends.

Dear God,

And God, please help me to tell Ben that I broke his guitar strings.

I didn't want to tell him about it but I think he knows.

Help Ben forgive me. He's the best brother in the whole world.— even if he does smell sometimes.

Love, Tyler

Therefore confess your sins to each other and pray for each other. . .The prayer of a righteous man is powerful and effective.

James 5:16

Bear with each other and forgive whatever grievances you may have against one another. Forgive as the Lord forgave you.

Colossians 3:13

None of us always does exactly what we should do all of the time. Unfortunately there are times when we actually do the exact opposite of what we should do, whether intentionally or unintentionally.

The temptation is to deny responsibility for our actions, but God teaches us the importance of taking responsibility for what we have done, confessing our sin, and asking for forgiveness.

When we confess our sin to God and to each other we are blessed with a cleansing and refreshing that is not experienced any other way.

We should live with a willingness to confess our mistakes whether they are sins or not and live with a willingness to forgive those who offend us in some way.

Dear God,

I know it must be hard on Mrs. Baker, babies cry A LOT, she misses Mr. Baker a lot too. But she still finds time to make us stuff. Don't tell Mom, but Mrs. Baker's fried chicken is way better.

Love, Tyler

With this in mind, we constantly pray for you, that our God may count you worthy of his calling, and that by his power he may fulfill every good purpose of yours and every act prompted by your faith.

2 Thessalonians 1:11

43

It is easy to get caught up in what we are personally dealing with and forget that others have struggles as well.

When we find ourselves focusing more on ourselves and our personal struggles, we should ask God to open our eyes wide to the needs of those around us.

We should take advantage of the love of those he has placed around us. We should allow our faith to be seen as we purposefully minister to others.

Dear God,

It's so cool that you're answering my letters.

You know the kid who delivers pizza to our house that I told you about? He used to just stare at me, and look really scared. Now he gets so excited whenever he sees me and talks to me and tells me things.

Love, Tyler

To the LORD I cry aloud,
and he answers me from his holy hill.

Psalm 3:4

Each of us is blessed far more than we realize. One of the greatest blessings we have is the privilege of communicating with God. He not only allows us to communicate with him, but he communicates with us as well.

Do we live in awe of who God is and all he does?

Never take for granted the blessing of prayer nor the magnificent ways in which God answers those prayers.

When we keep the eyes of our heart open we will see God working in all things, even in the things that seem insignificant to others. Write God some letters, share your heart with him, and expect him to answer — he will.

Dear God,

The pizza delivery kid said he thinks that he might want to become a doctor some day to help kids like me with cancer. Yep, You're so great!

Love, Tyler

I will be glad and rejoice in you;
I will sing praise to your name,
  O Most High.

Psalm 9:2

When is the last time you took the time to let God know how much you love him and thank him for all he has done?

God does more for us than we could ever imagine and we need to be committed to praising and thanking him regularly.

We should live with a grateful heart and consistently share our heart with God.

Having trouble thinking of things for which to thank and praise God? Try the "Alphabet Method." Go through each letter of the alphabet and name something for which to either thank or praise God. Name each thing as a prayer of thanksgiving or praise to God. Even better, write these things down and keep the list to refer to any time you need a reminder of God's faithfulness and awesome power!

Dear God,

I think I'll be seeing you soon.
I'm not feeling better like I
used to.

Love, Tyler

Be strong and take heart,
all you who hope in the LORD.

Psalm 31:24

I have fought the good fight, I have
finished the race, I have kept the faith.

2 Timothy 4:7

One day each of us will have our life on earth come to an end.

Many people come to the end of their earthly existence with regrets and fear.

Those who are Christians have a calm assurance that they will be with God and they will have no fear of facing what lies ahead.

When our hope is in the Lord we have the certainty of knowing we will be with him for all eternity.

Just as the Apostle Paul shared in 2 Timothy that he had fought the good fight, finished the race, and kept the faith, so too can we share the same message.

We should live with our hope and faith securely placed in the Lord so that when we face death we can do so with a peaceful and confident assurance.

Dear God,

Before I die, I'm wondering if you can help my friend Mr. Brady. He is so cool and he has a boy, but I don't think they see each other. Just like me and my dad. But Mr. Brady lives closer to his boy. Could you tell Mr. Brady's heart that it's going to be okay? And tell him you love him? And that his little boy does too?

Love, Tyler

This is how God showed his love among us: He sent his one and only Son into the world that we might live through him. This is love: not that we loved God, but that he loved us and sent his Son as an atoning sacrifice for our sins. Dear friends, since God so loved us, we also ought to love one another.

1 John 4:9-11

One of the great joys of being a child of God is the pleasure found in praying for and helping others.

Who do you know that you need to pray for? What are their needs?

God wants us to be "others-focused" rather than "self-focused."

It's fine to pray for our own needs, but God gave us a sensitive heart and a love for others so we could bring them before his throne in prayer.

God loves you and he loves those around you. Be committed to praying for those God allows you to know and always seek to guide them to the love of God.

54

Dear God,

Please Lord, help her find her way
back to you. Open her eyes to your love.

Love, Olivia

And so we know and rely on the
love God has for us.

1 John 4:16

. . . I trust in your unfailing love;
my heart rejoices in your salvation.

Psalm 13:5

God allows each of us the opportunity to know and love him. If we do know and love God, there are unfortunately times in our life when we turn away from him.

We need to continually rely on the love of God and when we have times of doubt and discouragement we need to come back to his side.

The best thing we can do for a fellow believer is to pray for them to come back to a close walk with the Lord.

Isn't it encouraging and awesome to know God's love for us is unfailing and unending? No matter how far we have turned away from God, he is waiting with open arms and an unconditional love and forgiveness for us.

Rejoice in His glorious and eternal salvation!

Dear God,

It's so much fun being your warrior. Mr. Perryfield was right. Is there anything you can do about that Green Goop? Do you think I can wear my eyebrows in Heaven?

Sam's going to need another friend you know. Someone she can take care of. Someone who likes to climb trees.

Love, Tyler

When the angel of the LORD appeared to Gideon, he said, "The LORD is with you, mighty warrior."

Judges 6:12

Everybody needs to know they have a purpose in life. Do you know your purpose in life?

God created each of us as a special, unique individual for the purpose of having a relationship with him. He created other people for the same purpose. Look at others as people created by God for the purpose of knowing God.

We also need to realize that every difficulty we face is an opportunity for us to be a warrior for God and honor him by what we say and do.

Anyone can have a good attitude when things are going well, but it takes a special person to shine brightly during the dark times of life. We should commit ourselves to being the faithful servant God calls us to be.

Dear God,

Thank you for watching over Mr. Baker. He's gonna love seeing his new little boy.

Love, Tyler

Sons are a heritage from the LORD,
children a reward from him.

Like arrows in the hands of a warrior
are sons born in one's youth.

Blessed is the man
whose quiver is full of them.

They will not be put to shame
when they contend with their enemies
in the gate.

Psalm 127:3-5

It is a blessing to know God is watching over each of his children wherever they are. Just as God enjoys his children so too do we love the privilege of being with our children.

We should live with an ever-present awareness of God's presence with us wherever we are, and faithfully pray for others to realize God's presence with them as well.

Never take for granted the blessing of your children. Love them and let them know they are loved each and every day.

Dear God,

And take care of all the other soldiers and help the families who already have somebody up there with you.

Love, Tyler

Greater love has no one than this, that he lay down his life for his friends.

John 15:13

He defends the cause of the fatherless and the widow . . .

Deuteronomy 10:18

There are people who place their lives on the line for us every day of the year. Many have given their life that we might enjoy the freedom we have.

One of the best things we can do is pray for those who serve our nation. We can also pray for the families who are left behind while fathers and mothers, husbands and wives, and sons and daughters are sent around the world.

Be faithful to pray for those who serve in the military and for those who have lost loved ones.

Dear God,

I know you're in control of everything.

Love, Tyler

I know that you can do all things;
no plan of yours can be thwarted.

Job 42:2

And we know that in all things God
works for the good of those who love
him, who have been called according to
his purpose.

Romans 8:28

It is an incredible comfort to know that God is in complete control.

This does not mean God causes everything to happen, but he is sovereign and nothing happens without him allowing it to happen.

When we live with the assurance of God's preeminence and majesty we are able to face anything that comes our way because we know that he has the ability to work everything out for good in our life.

We should place our faith solely in God every moment of our life and in every situation we encounter.

Dear God,

Tyler was the best friend ever.
I didn't get to tell him but
when we prayed with Alex, I
asked you to come into my
heart too. I know now, I have
forever-lasting life.

Love, Samantha

For God so loved the world that he gave
his one and only Son, that whoever
believes in him shall not perish but have
eternal life.

John 3:16

The greatest gift we can give a friend is to share with them how they can know God. The gift of salvation is provided by God to all who place their faith in his Son Jesus Christ.

We do not always know how God is using us but if we will remain faithful we can trust God to do incredible things in and through our life.

When someone receives Jesus as their Lord and Savior they have the promise of eternal life from God himself. We should allow God to use us to help others know how they can have a life changing relationship with Jesus Christ.

72

73

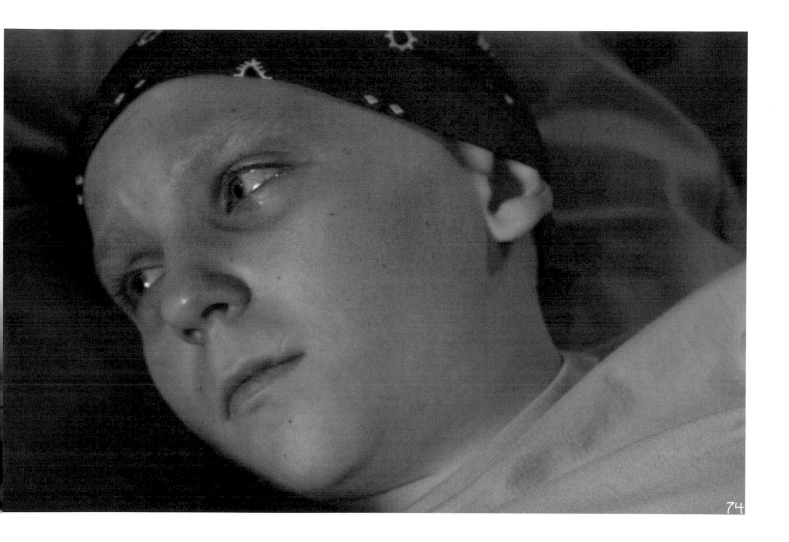

74

Dear Child of Mine,

I love you with a love that is deeper and wider than any love you will ever experience. Stay close to me and rest in me and my love for you. I have chosen to use you for my glory. Begin to see yourself as I see you – my precious child whom I have forgiven and for whom I have incredible plans. Get ready for the most exciting journey of your life as you continue to walk with me.

Love, God

But God demonstrates his own love for us in this: While we were still sinners, Christ died for us.

Romans 5:8

"For I know the plans I have for you," declares the LORD, "plans to prosper you and not to harm you, plans to give you hope and a future."

Jeremiah 29:11

The most wonderful relationship you will ever have is the eternal relationship of knowing and loving God. When you have that phenomenal relationship you are guaranteed forgiveness and a wonderful future.

This does not mean that everything that happens to you will be a "good" thing, but it does mean that God has a plan to bless you with both abundant life and everlasting life.

This relationship begins on the earth and continues for all eternity in heaven. You are a child of God and you should live like you are his child every day.

THE MAKING OF THE MOVIE
letters to God

Capturing Clip – NOW CAPTURING (press 'esc' to stop)

HEAVEN on EARTH

78

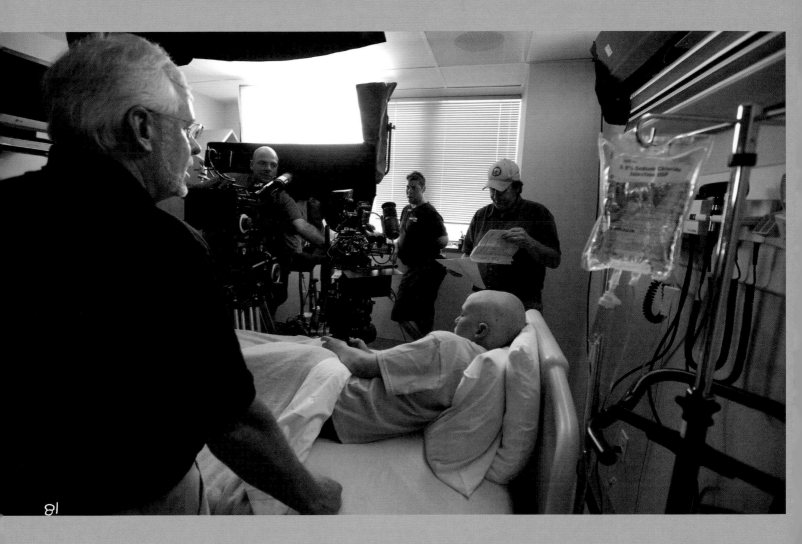

85

89

90